ROLAND M. TENNYSON

REBIRTH OF TENNYSON

KS

Kravitz & Sons

Kravitz and Sons LLC
204 E Arlington Blvd. Suite B
Greenville, NC 27858

Published by Kravitz and Sons LLC.

ISBN: 979-8-89639-382-5 (sc)
ISBN: 979-8-89639-381-8 (e)

Title of Contents

Rebirth of Tennyson
Is a collection of poems
Writen by Roland Mathew Tennyson
Ironically while reading
The biography of Alford Lord Tennyson
I found that both he and I
Were barn on August 6th
This gave me the title to my poetry book
These poems were inspired
By events in my life
Such as
Spending two and one half months in a coma,
Being rejected by close family members,
Having five open-heart operations,
And being told that I was mentally retarded and that
I would never read past a third grade level,
And the list goes on
But that's another story
In a biography I plan to publish within the next year.
Despite all my trials and tribulations
Through prayer, faith, and the grace of God
I can say I got my high school diploma,
Went to college and got my associates degree
And graduated top of my class with a 4.0GPA
I pray that this book and also the biography I plan to publish
In the near future will inspire you to learn
That all things are possible through Christ who strengthens you
I hope you enjoy this book.
God Bless

My Lesson

Even though this life gets hard
I trust you through it all.
When I need help, it's you I call
Father in Heaven
You came to me when I was only eleven
Raised me from then till now
And many a times I ask myself how
Could one so perfect find favor in me?
You told me not a word said
It's my life they'd see
Believe cause it's true; he gave his life, his blood, his son to show his
love.
Lately, I've been thinking
Of the example you gave
Knowing fire next time instead of rain
And how I've got to make a change
I don't want to remain lost
Lord you paid the cost for my sins
So that I could live
You're beter than a friend
I can't explain what you mean to me
I know I'm not the same
And until my change comes
I must rely on you
Cause no one can love me the way that you do
Don't get me wrong it doesn't end here
I've cried so much I feel baptized in my tears
Thinking I won't last because of sin
But I tell you my friend he's coming again
Repent your sins it's the only way
To go with him in the sky
And not get left behind
The fear of the Lord is the beginning of knowledge

But fools despise wisdom
So the Lord will not hear
Their voice when they call him
So his counsel they will not receive
You will eat from your own fruit
And with that you cannot grow
But if you receive his words,
And treasure his commands within you
Then the growth begins
As you incline your ear to wisdom,
And apply your heart to understanding
As you cry out for power
You will lift up your voice for understanding
And search for it like hidden treasure
But you must be careful
To take the father on your journey
He guards the paths of justice, and preserves the way
Of his saints, you must understand
There's no other way.
Do not let mercy and truth forsake you
Write them on the tablet of your heart
And find favor and high esteem in the sight of God and man.
Fear the Lord and depart from evil
It will be health to your flesh and strength to your bones.
Happy is the man who finds wisdom,
and the man who gains understanding.
For its proceeds" are beter than the profits of silver and gold
It is more precious than rubies
And all the things you may desire cannot compare
Lengths of days are in his right hand,
And in his left riches and honor
His ways are ways of pleasantness, and all his paths are peace.
He is a tree of life to those who take hold of him,
And happy are all who retain him.

Ready for Love

I am ready for love
But it never comes
For the reason I am living
And giving my all.
I always seem to fall
Short of what you say is mine
But could never find.
Like a blind man
I can't see
Love is hidden from me.
Lonely seems to be
My destiny alone.
My own thoughts.
Trap me Like an animal
In a cage I want to be free,
To see love
But it never comes.
I must stay headstrong
Silenced by the price of love.
Invisible, you are the one,
Impossible to hear
What you say to me
Are you awake, are you aware
Are you anything?
Pictures, frozen in time
That I can see Could it be
Theirs no love
Out there
For me?
Force to believe this
I must be the one you forgot, because
They call goliath
And I wear the David mask

I guess the stones are coming
To fast for them now.
All the stones that are thrown
Are building up a wall
So strong
It will never fall.
And when I hear of love,
And pray for love I want a chance,
But it looks like This is something I will never experience
So hear I am
The invisible man
Invisible to you
And everybody, it seems I am ready for love
But it never comes So I look above
For answers
But they never come down
Now I feel lost Is this the cost?
I can't see?
Where are you?
I am ready for love
But it never comes.

A Leter to the Lord

O God, my God
Have mercy now
I have only faith
I do not know
Knowledge is of things I see
And yet I trust it comes from thee.
Forgive what seem like a sin in me,
Forgive my grief for one removed.
I am still your child.
Men say that you died for me,
I should require a sign
And if a bolt of fire would arrive this summer noon,
While I pray to you alone,
Think my belief would stronger grow
Is not my human pride brought low?
Forgive the wild and wondering cries,
But Lord I do not believe I was born to die.
Confusions of a wasted youth
Forgive me where I fail in truth.
The boasting of my spirit still
The joy I had in my free will.
Was a vision of sin.
And the mountains draw it from the heavens above
And I need truth
So I'll go there to get me some.
Such ability inside me,
Made to do anything.
But you see the weakness inside
That's why I need you by my side.
You think the signs would make a difference
You think fire next time instead of rain
Would cause me to make a change.
But Lord I need your hand

So I can live up to your master plan.
Clear my spirit and my mind,
Help me find that love I could never find.
Once I was blind
But now I see
That Lord you love
Has always been there for me

This Litle Girl

This litle girl
Will fill my world
With something worth more
Than diamonds and pearls.
Just the thought of you
Makes my heart melt
Cause I know I love you
More than life itself
And joy I felt The day I held you
In my arms
Keeping you safe
From all harm
In this world
This litle girl S
o precious and smart
And just like a work of art
You are precious to my heart
Just like a candle, lights up the darkness
So will my love Light your pathway
My prayers were answered
The day you were born
With God on our side
We can't go wrong Your smile can bring joy
To the saddest individual Thank you Lord
For my miracle
And all that comes with it
Jazmine
My world is bright
Now that you're in it.

One More Day

One more day Is all I need
To tell you I love you
With you daddy
Is were I want to be
But somewhere in the sky
You lye
And I must say goodbye
Why'd you have to die?
Why must I cry?
For one more day
With you When my tears
Don't seem to help
What I'm going through Is it true?
That the dead knows nothing.
It's true
The thought of you
Makes me feel something
Deep in my soul
I didn't want you to go
But with my life
I will show
You did well
The son of "Donald Edward Tennyson sr."
In my heart
You will always dwell.

My Fathers Place

I'd rather live life the right way
And find out there is no heaven,
Than to live life the wrong way
And find out there is.
But by faith we know
Theirs a beter place than here,
A place we don't have to fear.
Wisdom is the principle thing.
Therefore, get wisdom and deliver yourself,
Go and humble yourself.
The way of life winds upward for the wise
That he may turn away from hell below.
With your life you must show that Christ lives in you.
You must choose your path, right or wrong.
He has already promised victory to those who are his.
He has made it so simple, its rite there in his word,
Quite surely you can't expect to be saved by the words you have heard
From another,
My brother, you've got to read and study for yourself, do it now
There's not much time left.
The test is life and so many fail.
Thinking there's no way to be saved
Cause your living in sin, but again I tell you,
He died for everyone,
God loves the just and unjust
Just trust, he's all you need.
Repent and change your life around
It's not too late,
To secure your place in heaven
"My Father's Place."

Deception

Deception, a lesson
Taught to be a blessing
While your second guessing
And asking questions
Life keeps on passing you bye
Why try?
You did your best
Even though you didn't
Get a hundred on the test
You passed
But not glad
Because you know you could have done beter
You just got by
And that's not how you want to live your life
Doing just enough to get by
There's that lie deception tells
Knowing in the long run
Just enough is going to fail
You're being deceived
Why can't you see? And beter yet
Why can't you beat? No, wait, I see
Stand on your own two feet
And deceive the deceiver
Believe the believer
And see with your own eyes
The truth
The deceiver is you
Because no one can make you do what you don't want to do.

Thank You

Everything I am is because of you
You gave me life
So forever I am in debt to you
Father up above
Like a dove I want to fly
And at the end
In Christ I want to die
Despite my sin
With you I can live
I am a farmer
And its harvest season
Another reason to grow
Reason to show
How good you've been to me
Cause without you
I could never be
Time has change
I am no longer the same
Born into sin
So were do I begin
My writing is an art
I can't end before I start
Only I can feel
The pain in my heart
And when I open my eyes
I'm in the dark
But you told me I'm all right
Cause when I could not see
You're my eyes
And when I can't go on
It was you who carried me along
With you I am strong
But anxiety is what I felt

Because Christ is the teacher
And Satan is a cheater
And life is the test
But still I am blessed
With blessing I don't deserve What have I earned?
An eternity to burn I have a lot to learn
But I can study only
What's placed before me
My eyes are still looking
For someone to show me
What I can't show myself
But in time, I know
My heart With God is kept
This I know
Cause it was he who never left
It was I who crept away
And I pray words
You have no reason to hear
But every morning I rise
I know you hear me
Loud and clear.

The Truth

The Sabbath Day T
he seventh day
A blessed day
The only sanctified day
By God
So I find it odd
That you forget
When the word says remember
Why hinder yourself
If you need help
He's there
Everyone needs prayer
This is a day set aside
For you to spend time with the creator
You say love your mom
Well it was he made her
And you need to know
That in his laws
He made no exception
They are still relevant
To this day
Worshipping on Sunday
Thinking its o.k.
But when you look at your calendar
You realize
That Saturday is the seventh day

I Was There

All the pain
You went through
I went through
Because I was there
When you left
And went somewhere else
I was there
The fear of me
Not being there
Should never arise
Because whenever you needed me
I was there
By your side
I came to you
Looking for love
I thought we could have fun
But a man I am
A king at heart
So you tell me
Why you're so far?
Because of you
I am gone
In your heart
You know it's wrong
So until the day
We meet again
In my heart
You were my best friend
And you know I care
Because I was there.

King

Revealing reflection
Of me
In this mirror I see
A child not ready to grow
A child who doesn't know
The one starring back
Is the one he's looking at
But a reflection unmoved
Is a reflection unproved
The mirror can only show you
And it shows a lot
Whether you like it or not
He's waiting to reveal
All those dreams you have within
You have completed control
Of what that mirror shows
Complete control
Of the person molded
Holding his life
In his hands
Reflecting truth
Is what it will bring
You should see a king.

Heaven

Jazmine, you are my heaven
You're the reason why I work so hard
It's been hard not seeing your face
But believe me when I say
You're not the blame I love you so much
I wish that I could touch your face
And tell you how I feel
My heaven is so beautiful
But I can only dream
That you are here with me
In my arms
Sheltering you from harm
I am still your father and always will be
Your mom won't let me see you
Until she is comfortable with it
All I wanted to do was love you
And I tried so hard, but the more I tried
Made me realize that maybe it's a lie
I love my family that much is true
Kali, you have my heaven and it's on your terms
That I can see her
I guess this is my curse for loving you so much
My mistake
My death
Because without you and Jazmine
There's nothing left
If you need me I am hear (listen) to your heart
Cause mine stopped.

I'll Try

It's my time to rise
If not I'd rather die
Because I don't want to feel ashamed to cry
When I look into the eyes of my child
I don't want you to see a failure
When you look at Daddy
I want you to be happy
Again I see me getting less than what I put in
I need a friend
I never had that
But the fact remains
Maybe I'm the blame
But for you
It won't be the same
That I will die to gain
So in your heart I will always remain without pain
Is that O.K.? This I ask
Cause this maybe my last
To pass to you
Just to let you know
Daddy love you
You will always be in my heart
From the beginning you were always smart
And you mean so much to me
Stress in my life I never want you to see
I'm sorry I have to go away this time
But I'll come back beter
I promise I'll try

Purpose

Consider my afflictions
They continue this day
My soul is weary
And for deliverance I pray
For the Day of Atonement has arrived
And I no longer feel alive
I am a man of great wisdom
And in much wisdom is much grief
But how can this be?
You told me to open my eyes
But Lord, I cannot see
Walk by faith is what you told me
For it's not by sight
You cannot see the prize
And that's when you reminded me
The fight is not mine
Are not these scars mine?
Wounds of a troubled youth
How long will you forget me?
How long will you hide your face?
Through whose eyes have I seen all this pain?
Surely I'm not blind
Why have you allowed so much pain in my life?
Why was I chosen to be cursed on this earth?
Confirm my purpose
And lead me into truth I pray
Wash me thoroughly
That I may go with you
On that day.

Understanding the Point

I will speak in the anguish of my spirit
I will complain in the biterness of my soul
As the cloud is consumed and vanishes away
So is he that goes down to the grave
But don't wait for that day
It's not too late to turn it around
Turn that frown upside down
Commit your works to the Lord
And your thoughts will he established
Understanding is a wellspring of life
To him who has it
The heart of the wise teaches his mouth
And adds learning to his lips
If you can understand this
Then my point you will not miss
Striving for peace
Preparing for war
Millions fighting and don't know what for
Peace is achieved by those who seek it
Peace on earth only last for a season
And just like rain, pain won't last always
Heaven is the place were peace will remain
Everything that goes up must come down
Except when the Lord takes you to higher ground
And I found that true love is earned
A point you must learn
Deserving all praise
Because he loves us first
And just think
If it was the other way around.
Imagine the universe
With no planet earth.

Street Life

Why drink from my hand
Contagious as you think I am?
Why follow me to higher ground
Lost as you swear I am?
Don't judge me just because I live a street life.
And it's not just me cause I can see the others.
Consider this, your not fighting to win because
The batle is already won.
Your test and trails come to make you strong.
I know, it shows in the way I live this street life.
Just tilt my sun toward your domain
And you will see your cup runneth over again.
Close friends don't seem to understand
Problems in my life, so complex
Many say Who can comprehend?
Waiting on the edge
With this confused heart
Waiting for someone to save you from yourself
Out hear on the ledge dangling somewhere in the dark
Doubting if anyone cares.
Who am I to ignore what I am feeling inside,
It's stronger than the hands of fate.
It leads me to a sacred place.
Full of hope and strife.
So I can get off these streets
And live my life.

Responsibility

Combining life with struggle
Born to you a bundle of joy,
But how long will that joy last?
Past, present, or future,
It should remain the same.
Many play it like a game.
But we all know,
That in a game,
One must lose and one must win,
It can't be both.
But that's what you chose.
This joy has no fears
Even though it shed tears,
It's here and you can't give it back.
That's a fact
But is it a fact that you lack
The mental state to pay for that?
I hope you see the reality of what you've done.
Joy isn't always fun.
But you can't run. This is your responsibility.
Even though everything in life serves a purpose
I can't find a purpose for ignorance.
Insurance is something to fall back on,
Get some
Or there will be no more fun.

Advise From God

I came to you confused
You gave me guidance
And asked that I join the alliance
Still not perfect
But you told me not to hide it
Never look away
When times get ruff
Just pray
Because as long as your alive
He'll provide for your days
Lord hear my cries
I beg of you please
I've lived this long
And it hasn't been easy.
Son, the test will come
And you'll pass with flying colors
There's no need to cry
Cause your mine
Now watch your world rise
Cause in my hands
Death never comes
And you think its ruff now
The best has yet to come.

In Disguise

Angel in disguise
Why must you hide?
From these eyes
Looking for you again
My best friend
My only friend
I can't win
With you on the other end
Falling in love
And we both fell together
Let's pick up Were we left off
On another level
Both unique But so far
Are we seeing eye-to-eye when tear drops fall?
Can you hear me when I call?
Or do you listen at all?
My angel wouldn't hide
So maybe this is goodbye
But this can't be
I'm for you and you for me
Don't tell me I have to travel alone
Because without you I can't go on
I want to come home
I don't want to be alone.

In Your Eyes

In your eyes
I see beauty
Heaven is missing an angel
And she's here with me
In your eyes
There is no disguise
You're the one
I've been waiting for
All my life I see truth
Let's pray and ask God what we should do
Cause this feeling I don't want to lose
Your eyes are telling more
Than you are willing to say
I just want to know
Do you feel the same way?
In your eyes
I see life
Yours and mine
And there's so much more
Together we are one
Your eyes tell it well
Forever in my heart
There you will dwell.

Doesn't Mater

It doesn't even mater
What I'm going through
My heart left with you
Now I'm left to ponder through
A world on my own
In my life
Everyone's gone
And I'm all alone It doesn't mater
That I'm yours
Mom is miles away So what is she for?
I can't make it
So just call me near
Cause all this fear
Don't help dry my tears
My dear sweet
Why must I?
Keep the pain inside
When there's no place to hide
I'm asking why?
Can't I be by your side?
I need a friend
To begin
Before my end.

Left Alone

Life went on without me
When you left
And now that you're gone
I had to find a way to go on.
All the nights I cried.
Knowing that you expected me to die.
Exceeding all expectations
I am very much alive.
And doing well,
With this life that was given to me.
But drastic times calls for drastic measures,
And I must do beter.
I will expect nothing less.
I was a failure, a lost cause in the eyes of many.
But you want to return now that I have plenty.
And you want to get mad cause I won't give you any.
But that's life.
And I must live with this temporary happiness,
This temporary joy that you think is great.
Silently I pray for answers.
Cause there's nothing great about being alone,
With no one to call
Nothing keeping me company but these walls,
Waiting for my heart to be filled again.
I lack the social skills to make friends.
Cause theirs no one I can trust.
You must know that.
Cause in the heart of batle no one had my back.

In Your Eyes Too

In your eyes
I see beauty
Heaven is missing angel
And she's here with me
In your eyes
There's no disguise
You're the one I've been waiting for
All my life
In your eyes
I see truth
Let's pray and ask God what we should do
Cause this feeling I don't want to lose
Your eyes are telling more
Than you are willing to say
I just want to know
Do you feel the same way?
And I saw in your eyes
As they started to water
And it made me wonder
What could make such beauty cry?
As you looked in my eyes
So I turned to walk away
But there was something about her eyes
That made me stay
For hours I tried to figure her out
She wouldn't say a word
And I didn't know what that was about
As frustration started to build
I had nothing else to say
I knew I should have left
Not knowing all this time
The woman was deaf.

Love

Favor is deceitful
And beauty is vain
But a woman who fears the Lord
Shall be praised S
o lift her up
She deserves your love
Give it to her
And she will give you love in return
Learn your role
A true woman will show you how to grow
Tell you what you should know
Queen of the earth
She deserves more than hurt
Believing your lies
Denying a life
Now she struggles
Just to get by
And cries for help
And no one's there
But she still gets by
Truth is
She got a kid
And she won't let go
She asked the Lord for help
And his promise he kept
Trust in the Lord
And he'll do the rest.

Strength

I ran for so long
But you still kept me strong
Now I'm were I belong
You raised a man
Took my hand
And gave me a plan
Now I can
Watch as it unfolds
My life worth more than gold
Just as you told
You I hold
No longer on my own
You let me see So I could be
Who you wanted me to be
You I'll never leave
Thank you for the good
Running no more
Since you opened that door
Now I love you more and more
And now like a dove I sore
Lord it feels good to be yours.

New Love

It's my time
Seems like the wind is behind me.
I'll never stray
Ever since that day I felt you in my life.
But were are we going now?
I don't mind
As long as you lead
I'll follow behind.
The words you say
Are so loving
And I can't turn away.
I've, seen the light of my ways
I've censed a brand new day
And all I need is you right here by my side.
I've, seen the light of my ways
I've censed a brand new day
And all I need is you right here as my guide.

www.ingramcontent.com/pod-product-compliance
Lightning Source LLC
Chambersburg PA
CBHW051251120626
46547CB00014B/1900